BACCHAI

Euripides

BACCHAI

Translated by Colin Teevan

Introduction by Edith Hall

OBERON BOOKS
LONDON

WWW.OBERONBOOKS.COM

First published in this translation in 2002 by Oberon Books Ltd.
521 Caledonian Road, London N7 9RH
Tel: +44 (0) 20 7607 3637 / Fax: +44 (0) 20 7607 3629
e-mail: info@oberonbooks.com
www.oberonbooks.com

Reprinted in 2007, 2012, 2016

PB ISBN: 9781840022612
E ISBN: 9781849436144

Printed and bound by 4edge Limited, UK.

Visit www.oberonbooks.com to read more about all our books
and to buy them. You will also find features, author interviews and
news of any author events, and you can sign up for e-newsletters so
that you're always first to hear about our new releases.

Visit www.oberonbooks.com to read more about all our books and to buy them. You
will also find features, author interviews and news of any author events, and you can
sign up for e-newsletters so that you're always first to hear about our new releases.

Printed on FSC accredited paper

for Madeline

Contents

Introduction

BY EDITH HALL

In antiquity Euripides was famous for being the most accessible of the tragic poets, the one who made his Bronze Age heroes speak 'ordinary' dialogue, which could be understood as easily as contemporary vernacular by Euripides' own fifth-century BCE audience. Of all the tragedians it was Euripides who was said by Aristophanes the comic poet and the philosopher Aristotle to have invented 'domestic' tragedy and who really knew how to make his heroes and heroines sound *human*. His poetry was accessible, intensely *speakable*, and easily memorised: anecdote upon anecdote tells how ordinary ancient Greeks and Romans, not just professional actors, loved to learn passages of Euripides off by heart for their own amusement. But at the same time Euripidean poetry includes passages of elevated diction, and is often marked by his distinctive characteristics of multi-layered irony, wit, rhetorical precision, lyric virtuosity, sinuous versification, and colourful imagery. The modern translator of Euripides has, therefore, a frighteningly tough act to follow.

Aeschylus and Sophocles, the other two ancient Greek tragedians, have in recent decades been fortunate in the excellence of poets who have adapted some of their plays for performance in the English language. It is thus paradoxical that Euripides, whose *Medea* and *Trojan Women* are performed as much as any other Greek tragedy and are acknowledged as classics of world theatre, has attracted few outstanding English-language translations. Truly readable (let alone actable) versions of Euripides are thin on the ground. The apparently 'realistic' tone of much Euripidean dialogue has also meant that he has been far less likely to be realised in masks than either Aeschylus or Sophocles, whose apparently more formal poetry is perceived to be more suited to masked delivery. Playscripts susceptible to masked performance require very special qualities of rhythm, pace, diction and style, and a particular type of relationship between actor, costume and stage property. It is even more difficult to produce a playscript which can be delivered, according to the ancient Greek convention, by a chorus plus a cast of only three male actors sharing all the speaking roles between them. A major reason for the coherent vision and integrity of Colin Teevan's rendering of *Bacchai*, commissioned for performance by the National Theatre in London, is that at every stage in its evolution it has been envisaged as an acting text for realisation not only in masks, but (as in the original production of Euripides' masterpiece in 405 BCE) by no more than three actors.

In one of the most astonishing moments in world theatre, at the heart of *Bacchai*, Dionysus, the god of drama, becomes a stage director. In disguise as a mortal himself, he leads in Pentheus, king of heroic Thebes, arrayed in the feminine dress of a bacchant. After adjusting the transvestite monarch's hair, hemline, posture and (most importantly) his perception of reality, he charmingly escorts him out to the countryside to die. Dionysus is of course the theatrical star of this show-stopping scene, as he is protagonist of *Bacchai* as a whole: but he is simultaneously its author, costume designer, choreographer and artistic director.

King Pentheus is symbolic of the experience of every actor and every audience who has ever renounced 'reality' and participated in the mimetic journey into dramatic illusion, the mysterious act of complicity by which Dionysus conjures actor and audience together into the other times and other places he can create in his theatre. Pentheus is both actor and audience; himself in disguise, playing the role of female bacchant, he is in turn deceived by the false identity assumed by the apparent priest, his cousin and adversary Dionysus. Pentheus is in a state of trance; he thinks he can see two suns, two cities, and that his companion is a horned bull. His delusion is painful and belongs to the realm of the tragic; his transvestism and vanity are decidedly comic. Pentheus and Dionysus thus play out in front of the audience the very process of assuming an altered identity and with it a transformed consciousness – the process inseparably identified in Greek culture with Dionysus, the god who presides over the various delusions associated with wine, with madness, and with theatre.

In ancient Greece tragedies were performed, as in the production of *Bacchai* for which this translation was prepared, by only three masked male actors and a masked chorus. The actor of ancient tragedy had to be highly flexible, able to assume several different identities in the course of a single production. The transformation from Dionysus into Teiresias or Pentheus into Agave, often within only a few minutes offstage, was made possible by the masking convention, but was still extremely challenging. The protean ability of the expert player to assume multiple identities in the course of a performance was much admired by ancient theatre-goers, but was also regarded as a frightening, destabilising, and socially dangerous renunciation of identity, especially when it entailed visibly turning into a woman. Some ancient actors were specialists in youthful and female roles (it is likely that the actor playing Pentheus and Agave was one such); others were especially famed for their dancing, singing, or thrilling performances of 'messenger speeches'. In a form of theatre uninterested in realism of facial expression, the ancient actor was highly skilled at voice modulation, and must have been plausibly able to impersonate radically different types of voice in the course of a production. The ancient actor imitated his tutelary deity, Dionysus, who was a master of disguise and metamorphosis. Yet there can be no doubt that the playwrights and actors exploited the internal echoes, ironies and suggestive parallels which this distinctive performance convention made possible. If the same actor who plays Pentheus also plays his mother – indeed enters the theatre brandishing his mask, the synecdochic substitute for his head – the intimate family relationship, and thus the pathos of the infanticide, are immeasurably heightened.

Repeatedly this play asks its audience to meditate upon the nature and function of the dramatic mask which made the actor's serial metamorphoses physically possible and theatrically plausible. The word for 'mask' (*prosopon*) in ancient Greek had none of its connotations in modern English of concealment or dissimulation. It was the regular word for 'face' or 'countenance', with particular emphasis on the features, especially the eyes: the *prosopon* marked the identity of an individual as he or she existed in relation to others, not something which hid a private and inalienable self from public view.

In Greek myth and ritual the mask signifies change – it marks boundaries between one condition and another. Young people don masks for initiatory rituals over which Artemis presides, marking the passage from childhood to adulthood. The Gorgon's mask is a monstrous female visage of lethal power: to glimpse it is to pass from life to death. To be gazed upon by the mask of Dionysus is cross the threshold between sanity and madness, between the real and the unreal, whether in ecstatic rites or in the theatre. When an actor donned his mask at the festival of Dionysus he marked an eruption into the heart of public life of a realm of being totally alien to the everyday world of the city. In *Bacchai*, astonishingly, an actor must assume the mask of Dionysus himself, for the god of epiphany is the protagonist. As if inspired by the god's presence on stage, Euripides' poetry draws unusually self-conscious attention to the illusory nature of theatre. In all drama, then as now, actors and audiences must collude with Dionysus and allow themselves to be conjured into the 'other' world of theatrical illusion.

Colin Teevan's translation deliberately focuses on this profoundly self-conscious dimension of *Bacchai*, but only by drawing out in English what is already latent in the text. He pays attention to the suggestive ancient terminology relating to faces, masks, spectacles, epiphanies, and the act of viewing. He sometimes translates the ancient Greek for religious 'rites' and 'rituals' as 'dramatic rites'. Above all, he slightly adapts the tragedy's prologue and epilogue (the latter, in any case, is partly missing in the manuscript tradition and needs to be supplemented for performance); his purpose is to emphasise the audience's entrance into and exit from theatrical illusion.

In an ancient hymn to Dionysus, an older text even than the serial choruses in praise of Dionysus included in Euripides' *Bacchai*, the god is kidnapped by pirates who mistake him for a mortal; but when they try to tie him up the bonds miraculously fall from him and he turns into a lion. Dionysus is the most protean of all gods, constantly and menacingly playing with disguise and transformations of the self. The ancient tale uncannily foreshadows the afterlife of Dionysus and his master text, *Bacchai*, in academe and the theatre. Over time this god always breaks free from the chains of every monolithic theoretical model imposed upon him and turns into something else.

From Byzantine times onwards *Bacchai* has often been seen as the ultimate literary expression of a sacramental rite by which Dionysiac 'communicants' became like the god and even one with him by devouring the body of the sacrificial victim. It is a sacred pagan poetic narrative absolutely bound up with the rituals associated with this god of the Mysteries, who in Euripides' own time could offer his devotees the glittering promise of a blessed afterlife. Since Freud, however, it has been possible to interpret the play as a brilliant articulation of the dark unconscious desires of the human psyche – the erotic, cannibalistic and murderous urges which can scarcely be perceived and yet motor human relationships and experiences of self and other. In Pentheus' desire to cross the boundary distinguishing gender roles and voyeuristically participate in the female Bacchanalian rites, the play has further psychoanalytical reverberations. More recently the play's loudest resonances have been heard in more sociopolitical terms, for it enacts not only a primeval clash between two ethnic groups, Greek and Asiatic, but an occasion on which some women revolted against male authority and broke the bonds tying them to their narrowly domestic sphere in a patriarchal society. And yet the very appeal of *Bacchai*, which has transcended two and a half millennia and massive cultural differences, is actually due to its radical insusceptibility to any single interpretation. It is curiously amoral, neither endorsing nor repudiating the cult whose arrival in one ancient city it dramatises. It does not offer a single, simple way of understanding an incomprehensible universe. It simply stages one terrible occasion on which an introspective and xenophobic community resisted, derided, disrespected and excluded innovation and difference – ethnic, cultural, religious and psychological – and in consequence suffered catastrophe.

Polarisation of apparent opposites – Greek versus barbarian, man versus woman – was a structural characteristic of the ancient Greek world view. Yet Dionysus in *Bacchai* demonstrates to the shattered people of Thebes that conventional thinking is utterly inadequate to the cognitive and metaphysical task of understanding the workings of the universe. He proves that human perceptions of reality are fundamentally unreliable and that the truth can sometimes be better discovered through the illusion available in the theatre than by strict empirical inspection of the strictly observable world. He subverts binary thinking, inverts all hierarchies and confounds all reason. He may be worshipped in eastern lands, but his mother was a Theban Greek. He may allow the women of Thebes to question male authority, yet he ruthlessly sends them mad and destroys their lives in order to impose his own (far more stringent) authority instead. A male deity worshipped with images of erect phalluses, his masculinity is yet compromised by his long hair, delicate beauty and decorative clothing. Illicitly celebrated on the wild hillsides, he is the subject of an important established cult at the heart of the city. An immortal god millennia old, he is yet eternally youthful. He dissolves the difference between tragedy and comedy; his worship offers both transcendental ecstasy and the most terrifying of all violence – a parent's destruction of her child.

In *Bacchai* Dionysus liberates prisoners, deranges the rational, effeminises men, and with his earthquake visibly, manifestly intrudes the untamed verdant natural world into the brick-built, ordered interior of the supposedly 'civilised' city. In one of his last plays, produced posthumously after a long lifetime of thinking about the nature of theatre, Euripides created a tragedy proving that Dionysus, and our relationship to him, are ultimately unknowable. Apollo at Delphi famously told the ancient Greeks to 'know thyself'; in *Bacchai* Dionysus warns us to be aware that we do not and cannot really know ourselves or our universe at all.

Edith Hall
Professor of Classics and Drama,
Royal Holloway University of London

Characters

DIONYSUS

CHORUS
of Asian Women

TEIRESIAS

CADMUS

PENTHEUS

GUARD

HERDSMAN

SERVANT

AGAVE

SOLDIERS

This translation of *Bacchai* was first performed at the National Theatre (Olivier) on 8 May 2002, with the following cast:

DIONYSUS/TEIRESIAS/SERVANT, Greg Hicks

CADMUS/SOLDIER/HERDSMAN, David Ryall

PENTHEUS/AGAVE, William Houston

CHORUS, Nicola Alexis, Ewen Cummins, Lee Haven-Jones, Chuk Iwuji, Rebecca Lenkiewicz, Wendy Morgan, Richard Morris, Renzo Murrone, Stefani Pleasance, Margaret Preece, Marie-Gabrielle Rotie, Rachel Sanders, Geoffrey Streatfeild, Clare Swinburne, Jax Williams

Director, Peter Hall

Designer, Alison Chitty

Composer, Harrison Birtwistle

Lighting Designer, Peter Mumford

Movement Director, Marie-Gabrielle Rotie

Sound Designer, Paul Groothuis

Assistant Director, Cordelia Monsey

Company Voice Work, Patsy Rodenburg

Mask Maker, Vicki Hallam

Musical Directors/Musicians, Nikola Kodjabashia, Kawai Shiu

Musicians, Martin Allen, Rufus Duits, Alan Hacker, Belinda Sykes

A bare stage.

DIONYSUS

An empty space and all of you, and me.
And who am I? Dionysus son of Zeus;
God of the vine, god of dramatic rites,
God of the transformation from the humdrum
To the wild abandon of the play.
So let us play, so let us beat the drum,
I have returned to the city of my birth;
To the banks of this broad river,
To where the city ends and the wild begins,
A place poised between two worlds,
To where Semele, the daughter of the old king Cadmus,
My mother, bore me through the lightning fire.

I have come home and taken human form
So my true nature be made manifest,
So that I might suspend the disbelief
Of all who dare not believe in me.
Let's play, I said. Look and you'll begin to see.

My mother's tomb, standing where she was struck down.
See how it smoulders still from the thunderbolt of Zeus;
Hurled by his wife Hera in bittersweet revenge
For all these love affairs with mortal girls.
See too how old Cadmus preserves as sacrosanct
The place where his daughter, my mother, died.
And look! my contribution; luscious vines.
You see? You begin to hear the drumbeat?
The drumbeat I first fashioned in the East,
In the depths of darkest Asia.

He dances.

I left the gold rich lands of Lydia
And Phrygia, for Persia's upland plains,
Then on to towered Bactria I danced.

1

The lands of the Medes held no fear for me
As I described an incandescent arc
Across the deserts of Arabia.
The East soon came to know my mysteries,
Half the known world now dances to my drum.
As for the other half, as for you…

    He stops dancing.

This city here shall be the first
Of all the western world to cry my cry,
And dress themselves in dappled skins of deer,
And raise the ivy-covered club, my sacred shaft.
And why? Because the three sisters of my mother,
Ino, Autonoe and Agave,
Have dared declare that I, Dionysus,
Was not fathered by my father Zeus,
But say that my own mother Semele
Was seduced by some mere mortal.
What's more, these aunts of mine say
That it was for the spreading of this lie
Of divine rape, that Zeus himself killed my mother.
Well, for their impudence I've driven them,
Raving from their homes, to Mount Cithairon,
Ranging wild, dressed only in the skins of beasts.
They'll dance my dance and cry my cry, they'll do my rites;
Mothers, daughters, wives, sisters, serving girls
One and all, regardless of their station,
Living rough amidst the rocks and pines
Under a roofless sky. This city shall learn,
Whether it might wish to learn or not,
The full dramatic rites of Dionysus.

Cadmus has long since relinquished rule here
In favour of his grandson Pentheus.
Cousin Pentheus who makes war on me,
Pours me no libations, nor remembers me in prayers.
But he shall believe. All shall believe.

And if he tries to force his women down,
I'll lead down on him such a ragtag army
Of wild and frenzied women he will relent.
For this reason I play the part
Of a priest of Dionysus,
Chief celebrant of my own rituals.
And this my sisterhood of followers,
Who've marched with me from Asian Phrygia
And Lydian Mount Tmolus –

The stage is dressed. Enter the CHORUS.

– Sound the sound,
Beat the Barbarian drum, my women,
With the beat first begun by Mother Earth.
Make the palace of this Pentheus pound;
This whole city shall come bear witness to me.
I'll go join their women on Mount Cithairon.

Exit DIONYSUS.

CHORUS
From Phrygia,
From Lydia,
We followed Dionysus' drum.
Hard work
Is sweet work
In honour of Semele's son.
You on the street,
You in the house,
Come show the reverence due:
Our song
Is the true song,
We sing it now for you.

Blessed she who knows
The mysteries of the Gods,

Who lives the life devoted,
Who lets her spirit soar and so unify
In wild mountain dancing,
Ordained by Mother Earth
Who, with the ivy-covered shaft
And ivy-plaited hair,
Raised the young Dionysus.

Go, you Bacchai, go!
Let our priest of Dionysus
Lead out from deepest Asia
To the wide streets of the West,
Dionysus, son of Zeus.

Tell of Dionysus,
Tell how cracked from his mother's womb
By the lightning bolt of Zeus,
How Zeus hid him in his thigh,
Closed fast with golden pins,
Out of Hera's vengeful sight.
So was the bull-headed God,
Who wears the wreath of snakes,
Born as the Fates decreed.

Put on wreaths of ivy,
Pull down sprays of pine
And branches of the oak.
Come, come into bloom
My wild mountain flowers.
Put on the skins of deer,
Plait your hair with flowers,
Hold high your sacred shafts:
All here shall join the dance.
Follow the priest of Dionysus
To the woods and to the mountains
Where the God pricks the women wild.

Secret cave of Crete,
Secret cradle of Zeus,

Where first the Courbantes
Drew tight the goatskin on the drum
And at once began the beat,
Which mated with the serpent sound
Of Phrygian pipes,
Made the first song of all songs.

What joy upon the mountains,
What ecstasy on high,
When dressed in skins of deer,
You join the sacred hunt,
And fall upon your prey,
And rip a flailing limb,
And taste the still warm flesh
Of a still-living mountain goat.

Then spills the earth with milk,
Spills with wine, with honey
Of wild bees, it spills forth:
You are now Bacchai.
And the priest lifts up
His ivy-covered club
Which burns with smoke as sweet
As Asian frankincense.
You run and dance around
His now streaming torch,
His hair a shock of flames
As he roars you on;
'Go you Bacchai, go!
With the gold of Mount Tmolus
Beating in your veins,
With the booming drumbeat
Beating in your heart.
Sing Evoe to Dionysus,
Sing Evoe to the god,
Sing with my faithful Phrygians
To the serpent-sounding pipes;

In beat to your feet
As you wander wide
Through wild mountain glens.'

And you are as carefree
As the foal who caracoles
Around its mother in the spring.

Enter TEIRESIAS.

TEIRESIAS

Who guards the gate? Call Cadmus from his house,
The son of Agenor who from Sidonia
Came here, slaughtered the serpent, sowed its teeth
And reaped a city. Call him and tell him
That old blind Teiresias is here. Now.
He'll know why I've come; we made a deal.
Though I am old and he is older still,
We wear the wreath of ivy on our head;
The dappled skins of deer upon our back;
And in our hands hold high the sacred shaft.

Enter CADMUS.

CADMUS

Friend, from within my house I heard your voice,
The wise words of the wisest of old men,
And I've come with all the God requires.
And so I should since he's my daughter's son –
A God in the family is no bad thing,
No bad thing at all. Where shall we go dance?
Where must we go to shake our old grey heads
And rattle these old sacks of shrunken bones,
And beat the ground in youthful exultation,
Though I am old and you are older still.
Tell me Teiresias, where shall we go?
I could dance all day to the god's drumbeat.
Such a sweet release to forget the years.

TEIRESIAS
Though younger than you, I feel younger still
I too intend to dance.

CADMUS

But where, old

friend?
Here?

TEIRESIAS
No. Up on Cithairon.

CADMUS

The mountain?
Perhaps we'd better take a horse and cart?

TEIRESIAS
That would not show the God due reverence.
With bare feet upon bare earth must we go.

CADMUS
Though I am old, you are older still, and blind,
I'll have to guide you.

TEIRESIAS

The god shall

guide me.

CADMUS
If you insist.

TEIRESIAS
I do, and so does he.

CADMUS

I see.
Are we the only men to dance with him?

TEIRESIAS
The only men who see things as they are.

CADMUS
Let's go then. Take my left hand in your right.

TEIRESIAS
Together they shall make a perfect pair.

CADMUS
Mortals defy the gods at their own risk.

TEIRESIAS
Nor should man try to rationalise the gods.
The age-old beliefs of our forefathers
Can't be constrained within the narrow frame
Of words. Not even by the sharpest minds.

CADMUS
Some might say it is embarrassing
For old men to dance with ivy on their heads.

TEIRESIAS
What is time to gods? Therefore, what is age?
Both young and old alike must join the dance.
He demands that all hold him in honour,
As community, no man set apart.

CADMUS
Though you see clear the future and the past,
To the present you're quite blind, Teiresias,
And Pentheus comes towards us presently,
The son of Echion to whom I gave
My power in this land. And I need be no prophet
To divine his fury. He is breathing fire.

Enter PENTHEUS.

PENTHEUS

I leave the city for three short days
And am no sooner on the road but hear
That all our women have abandoned house and home
And taken to the mountains in nothing
But the skins of beasts and gad about
Dark forests in demented dancing,
In the name of some new-fangled cult
Of Dionysus. Furthermore I hear
The chief practice of this cult consists
Of drinking quantities of wine then sneaking
Off to slake the thirsts of male concelebrants.
They might see this as some sort of sacred rite
Of this self-styled god, but from what I see
They are driven not by duty but desire.
Those whom I've caught I've bound both hand and foot
And placed under heavy guard in prison,
Those who remain at large I will hunt down.
That includes Agave, my own mother,
Her sisters Ino and Autonoe,
Mother of my dead cousin Actaeon.
With hunter's net and manacles of iron,
I will stop these evil rites from spreading.
I've also heard that some Asian foreigner,
Masquerading as a kind of priest,
With big brown eyes and long, golden hair
– Too womanish to be a proper man–
Keeps constant company with our women
And with his song and dance leads them astray.
If I catch him within my city's walls
I'll soon stop his drumstick drumming
I'll cut off those long, gold, blond locks of his.
He's the one who claims that Dionysus
Is a god hatched from the thigh of Zeus.
Dionysus is no god, nor son of god,
But died in the womb in the lightning blast

That killed his mother, my aunt, Semele;
Struck down for the boast that she'd lain with Zeus.
The gods will always punish arrogance.
And this foreigner, like Semele, will pay.
And what's this? Another wonder! Our prophet
Teiresias dressed in the dappled deerskin
And grandfather with a wand of ivy?
Has the whole city gone completely mad?
You make me sick, you make me want to laugh.
You make me want to laugh till I throw up.
So many years and yet so little sense.
Take off that wreath of ivy grandfather!
Throw down that silly stick! Do what I say!
I blame you for all of this Teiresias,
You hope by the invention of new gods
To expand your business in burnt offerings.
If it weren't for your wrinkles and grey hair
I'd bind you like the women, hand and foot,
For spreading such unseemly practices.

CHORUS

Impious man! Son of snake-skinned Echion,
Do you not fear the Gods? Have you no shame?
To speak in such a way to old Cadmus?
He sowed the serpent's teeth from which your city sprang!
Do you have no respect for family?

TEIRESIAS

When the wise man has a sound argument
The words come easily, their meaning clear;
You, however, give the impression of a sense
Which, when one tries to grasp it, vanishes.
Whatever earthly powers a man might have,
They are nothing if he can make no sense.
As regards the power of this 'self-styled god',
As you call him, my words cannot express

How great it shall extend through all the world.
There are two gods, sir, primary to man:
The one, Demeter, Gaia, Mother Earth
– Whatever name you may wish to give her –
From her comes the grain that makes the bread of life.
The other is the son of Semele,
Who bestowed on man the gift of wine
That makes endurable this rack of life
And grants sweet release from daily cares;
And when we drink his wine, we drink of him.
Through this gift is man restored and renewed.
As for the tale of how Dionysus
Was incubated in his father's thigh,
A tale you scoff at, I will tell you, sir:
As Semele lay dying from the bolt,
Hurled at her in jealousy by Hera,
Zeus snatched the still-live foetus from her womb
And brought it to Olympus, but Hera
Wished to throw the infant back down to earth.
So Zeus, as gods are apt to do, hatched a plan.
He fashioned from the clouds an image
Of the infant which he gave to Hera
As a pledge for his future fidelity.
So was the real child saved from Hera's wrath –
Brought up in Nysa, I believe, by nymphs.
But because the old word 'mayros' for thigh,
Resembles the word 'homayros' for pledge,
As in the pledge that Zeus had given Hera,
Over time, as the story was retold,
Men came to believe that Dionysus
Gestated in the thigh of his own father.
He has the power of prophecy as well
For, when one performs his whirling dances,
Dionysus enters whole one's body
And one can divine all that is to come.
Nor is he absent when it comes to war.

You know the scene, your army all drawn up
And primed for battle suddenly takes flight,
Terror struck before a single spear is thrown;
This madness comes direct from Dionysus.
And in time he shall be seen in triumph
Standing high upon the rocks of Delphi.
Listen to what I'm saying, Pentheus,
Physical force will not change men's beliefs.
Do not act upon an inclination
That proceeds from an overheated mind.
Welcome the God, make him offerings,
Put a wreath upon your head and join the dance.
Dionysus does not make immodest
The desires of any woman,
It's woman's nature, not a god, that determines
How a woman will or won't behave.
For, when it comes to do his rites and dance,
She who is by nature modest, stays so,
And she who's not, will have no modesty to lose.
Do you not see? Just as it pleases you,
When people sing the praise of Pentheus,
So does a god delight to hear his name
Ring out in music, story and in song.
Therefore Cadmus and I, despite your scorn,
And despite his age, will join in the dance
And wear the ivy wreath upon our heads.
It is our duty. I'll not fight a god.
I'll listen to your arguments no more.
You are sick, and the sickness clouds your judgement.

CHORUS

You show wisdom and humility, old man;
To honour this god as a great god;
There is no greater god than Dionysus.

CADMUS

My son, Teiresias gives good advice.
Dwell within the temple of our beliefs,
Not in the wilderness that lies beyond.
Your senses have quite taken leave of you,
For even if this god is not a god,
Why not play the part of a believer
And put on the appearance of a faith,
So Semele, as mother of the god,
Be honoured and, by extension,
Earn us honour too. Remember Actaeon,
Devoured by dogs that he himself had raised
Because he boasted far and wide
That he was the greatest hunter of them all?
Greater than the goddess Artemis?
Do not suffer as he suffered my son.
Let me wreath your head with ivy,
Let us all go give the god some honour, eh?

PENTHEUS

Don't touch me! Don't pollute me with your madness!
Go, grandfather, go dance your stupid dance.
As for your instructor in idiocy,
He shall receive a lesson in justice.
Guards, go directly to this old fraud's home,
Smash up his pots and pans of prophecy
And throw his priestly frocks into the river.
Take crowbars and topple down his walls until
Not one stone still stands upon another.
As for the rest of you, search the city,
Hunt down this foreigner who dares infect
Our women's minds and bodies and our beds.
Catch him, tie him up, then bring him here to me.
Him too shall I educate in justice,
By stoning him to death. He'll soon regret
The day he brought his filthy foreign practices

To our city in the West.

Exit PENTHEUS.

TEIRESIAS
Heedless man! You don't know what you're saying.
Before you were simply being unwise,
Now you are quite mad. Let us go pray, Cadmus,
That he might find a cure for his affliction,
And that the god might not blame his actions
Upon the city as a whole. Let us go,
You support me and I will support you;
It is embarrassing when old men stumble,
Though all that shall fall will fall.
I put my faith in Dionysus, son of Zeus.
Pentheus connotes 'penthos' meaning grief,
I hope not more grief for your house, Cadmus.
I say this not by way of prophecy,
But guess from what this grievous fellow says;
Unwise words always lead to unwise deeds.

Exit CADMUS and TEIRESIAS.

CHORUS
Hear this, Demeter, goddess of the cornfield
Hear this, Gaia, mother of the earth,
Hear what this earth-born Pentheus
In profanity and proud opposition,
Said of the son of Semele.
Dionysus,
Whom the gods themselves rank
Most blessed of their number.
Dionysus,
Who inspires both gods and men
With his abandoned dance.
Dionysus,
Who leads the laughter with his pipe

And with his gift of wine
Calms all mortal cares.
And it is Dionysus who,
When down on the earth we lie,
Wraps us in the cloak of sleep.

The unwise tongue unwinds a tale
That terminates in grief.
But, reverence of the gods
Brings grace, binds homes,
Families and cities all together.
Do the gods their rites
And they'll do right by you.
Though living in the heavens,
They watch the deeds of man.
Cleverness is not wisdom
And he who's short of wisdom
Will make shorter his own life.
While he who strives for greatness
Will miss what is to hand.
But what use are such words
To a man who will not listen?

Let us go east to Cyprus,
The isle of Aphrodite,
Where Eros weaves enchantment
On all who seek love there.
Or north to Mount Olympus
Where the hundred-mouthed rivers meet.
Lead me there, Dionysus,
Lead on my soul in ecstasy
To where grace might be found.
Our god, the son of Zeus,
Rejoices in the pleasure
All who follow him will find.
He is the friend of Eirene,
The Goddess of Peace, the goddess

Who keeps safe young men,
And his gift he gives alike
To all both rich and poor;
Release from mortal care.
But he who spurns his gift
The god, our god, will crush.

There is more wisdom in the common man's belief
Than the decrees of mighty kings.

*Enter GUARD and SOLDIERS from city, escorting the captive
DIONYSUS as a priest. Enter PENTHEUS from the palace.*

GUARD

Pentheus, here is your wild animal.
He was not hard to run to ground.
Even when I cornered him he did not try
To bolt for it but, without persuasion,
Calmly offered us his hands and laughed.
I'm sure I've never caught so tame a thing.
I told him straight, 'My friend, it is not me
Who ordered this arrest, but Pentheus.'
He just told us to do as we'd been bid.
And that's another thing, those few women
You caught and clapped in irons in jail are gone.
Their leg irons just opened, fell at their feet
And the door bolts shot back all by themselves.
They're all running back now to the mountain,
Jumping for joy, giving thanks to their god.
Many are the wonders this man here works.
Though what must now be done is up to you,
Of course, I –

PENTHEUS

                    Shut up. Bring him here to me.
Untie him. He'll not run. He knows the class
Of hunter who has trapped him in the net.

16

Besides, these long locks and these rosy cheeks
Would suggest our friend here's no prize fighter.
Your body is not entirely unattractive,
To a woman's taste at least, which I believe
To be the purpose of your visit here.
Look, this skin's not felt the sting of sun rays.
This man walks in shadows not in light
And hunts the dark secrets of Aphrodite,
Using his youthful beauty as the bait.
But I'll reveal the truth so all shall see through him.

DIONYSUS
Have your truth. Look through me. I've nothing to hide.

PENTHEUS
We will see about that.

DIONYSUS
                                        We will see only
When we can see.

PENTHEUS
                                        Well you see here: where
are you from?

DIONYSUS
You have heard of Mount Tmolus I presume?

PENTHEUS
In Lydia.

DIONYSUS
                    Lydia was my home.

PENTHEUS
Why then bring your practices to my home?

DIONYSUS
Dionysus, son of Zeus, compelled me.

PENTHEUS

Does Zeus now have the power to make new gods?

DIONYSUS

Not entirely. Your aunt gave him a hand.

PENTHEUS

Zeus killed Semele for spreading that same lie.

DIONYSUS

As I said, she did lie. She lay with Zeus.

PENTHEUS

Well how did my 'dead cousin' compel you, then?

DIONYSUS

He came to me and told me face to face.

PENTHEUS

Explained all his mysteries, just like that?
Speak straight without any deviation.

DIONYSUS

He who believes needs no explanation.

PENTHEUS

What's the worth in believing worthless things?

DIONYSUS

Much worth, but not worth telling you, it seems.

PENTHEUS

The more you say, the more I am intrigued.

DIONYSUS

To be intrigued is still not to believe.

PENTHEUS

Face to face, you said, how did he appear?

DIONYSUS

He appeared there as he now appears here.

PENTHEUS

While you appear to riddle to deceive me.

DIONYSUS

A riddle only to the man who disbelieves me.

PENTHEUS

Well then why does Dionysus not appear before me?

DIONYSUS

You will see him only when you can see.

PENTHEUS

Tell me, is this the first place to which you've come?

DIONYSUS

All foreign lands now dance to his drum.

PENTHEUS

That is why they are foreign and we're not.

DIONYSUS

Race matters to this god, not a lot.

PENTHEUS

And you perform these practices at night?

DIONYSUS

Man's true nature's seen in darkness not in light.

PENTHEUS

While darkness shrouds a woman's true duplicity.

DIONYSUS

Duplicity is not found at night exclusively.

PENTHEUS

You'll pay for your daylight duplicity!

DIONYSUS

And you for your heedless impiety!

PENTHEUS

You've a foolhardy tongue on you, my foreign friend.

DIONYSUS

Well, what punishment have you planned for me?

PENTHEUS

First I shall cut these long, blond locks of yours.

DIONYSUS

My hair's as sacred as Dionysus'.

PENTHEUS

Then I'll relieve you of that silly stick.

DIONYSUS

This is the sacred shaft of Dionysus.

PENTHEUS

Then I shall throw you in the common jail.

DIONYSUS

He'll set me free should I but wish it so.

PENTHEUS

He'll come down from on high and rescue you?

DIONYSUS

He's here, he sees and suffers all I do.

PENTHEUS

He's here, is he? Why can't I see him then?

DIONYSUS

Because your ignorance has blinded you.

PENTHEUS

Seize him! This man insults me and my city.

DIONYSUS

I'm not the man that needs restraining here.

PENTHEUS

Do it, guards! I've more authority than *him*.

DIONYSUS

You know not what you are, nor what you do.

PENTHEUS

I do. I'm the king. I am Pentheus.

DIONYSUS

Your name suggests grief. It will suit you well.

PENTHEUS

Throw him in the stables with the other beasts.
Let him teach them his foreign ways,
Let him see his true nature in the dark,
There let him dance there till he drops down in the shit!
He will respect the West before he dies.
As for those he has led into evil,
Take them to market to be sold as slaves,
Or to my own house, there to work the looms,
So their hands can no longer beat his drum.

Exit PENTHEUS.

DIONYSUS

I am ready. What have I to fear from you?
For what must now fall, will not fall on me.
Dionysus himself, whom you deny,
Shall see to that. He'll see to everything.

You wrong him when you wrong me, my friend,
Believe me.

Exit GUARD and SOLDIERS leading off the captive DIONYSUS.

CHORUS
Sweet river,
Offspring of the river god,
In your waters
You cooled the son of Zeus,
When he was snatched
From his mother's burning womb,
So that Zeus could then place him
In his thigh and sing:
'Come my child of fire
Be born from this male womb
You shall be made manifest
As a god to all world.'
Silent flowing waters,
When I come now to your banks
And wear the wreath of ivy,
And worship him in dance,
You shrink back from the shore.

City of the West
Why do you turn from me?
For by the taste of his dark wine
You'll come to know the truth.

What rage has this man of earth,
This Pentheus descended
From the earth-sown serpent's teeth,
This son of Echion the snake-skinned!
Wild-eyed, he seems
More animal than man.
Soon shall we too be bound
And, like our priest,
Thrown into the dark.

Dionysus don't you see
How your priest is wronged?
Dionysus don't you see
How your children suffer?
Come with your golden shaft,
Come down from Olympus,
From the sacred woods where Orpheus
Made the very trees resound with song
And led all wild animals
In the mountain dance.
Come down from your heights
Which ring to the Evoe
And crush this too proud man of earth.

Come make the river dance once more with joy.

DIONYSUS
(Off, as God.)
Io!
Hear me, hear my cry!
Io Bacchai! Io Bacchai!

CHORUS
What's that?
Who cries the cry of Dionysus?

DIONYSUS
I cry the cry!
I, the son of Semele,
I, the son of Zeus.
Io! Io!

CHORUS
Io! Io!
Our lord, our god.
Reveal yourself to us
And lead us in the dance.

DIONYSUS

Goddess of the earthquake,
Shake the table of the world.

Earthquake.

CHORUS

A! A!
The palace shall be shaken to the ground.
Dionysus is here.
Kneel down, kneel down women.
See the stone lintels split in two!
Our priest shall be freed. Listen!
The god's war cry from the house.

DIONYSUS

Come lightning fire and strike
The palace of this Pentheus
Down to the dust.

The shrine of Semele bursts into flames.

CHORUS

A! A!
And look! Do you not see? Flames!
Blazing from the tomb of Semele
Herself struck down by the fire of the gods.
Stretch your bodies on the earth.
Abase yourself.
Dionysus brings low
Those who seek the heights.

Enter DIONYSUS as priest.

DIONYSUS

Women, why are you so full of fear
Why lie upon the ground? Do you not see?
Dionysus has destroyed the palace.

Pick yourselves up and stop your trembling.
You of little faith to fear that Pentheus
Could contain the priest of Dionysus
Behind some makeshift prison walls.

CHORUS

It was for our safety that we feared.
But tell us what happened. How did you escape?

DIONYSUS

Without the slightest effort, that is how.

CHORUS

Did he not bind you fast both hand and foot?

DIONYSUS

It is he who is now bound in blindness.
He thought he'd hold me prisoner in his house,
He hoped to bestow on me a thorough beating,
Yet he did not lay a hand on me.
Instead, upon entering the stables,
He saw a bull and to this bull he ran,
Howling, panting with rage, spitting revenge,
And, grabbing the bull, bound it hoof to hoof,
While I sat by and watched most peacefully.
Then Dionysus really took control.
He shook the palace to its foundations,
And from the tomb of Semele sent flames
So Pentheus, thinking his house on fire,
Ran up and down calling for water
To be fetched up from the river right away.
All his slaves set about this pointless task,
While Pentheus, thinking that I'd run indoors,
Drew his sword and rushed inside after me.
But then the God himself, it seemed to me,
In the shape of a tremendous shadow
Cast from a cloudless sky, appeared.

25

So Pentheus rushed at it, a shadow,
And tried to stab it, thinking it was me.
Not content with this humiliation,
The god had further plans for punishment.
He toppled the palace of this Pentheus
Who dropped his sword then dropped to his knees, defeated.
The price of my imprisonment was high,
For him. Then I came here. A free man.
As for Pentheus, not that I really care
For Pentheus, but he too now comes this way.
Have no fear, I will weather his fury;
He who would be wise will keep his self-control.

Enter PENTHEUS.

PENTHEUS
Where is he? Where is that filthy foreigner
Who dares defy my justice? Ea! Ea!
What?! What's this?! In front of my own house?!
Standing as brazen as the day is long?!

DIONYSUS
Easy boy! Beware the beast you bark at!

PENTHEUS
But how? The guards? The chains? And you, you, you escaped?

DIONYSUS
I did tell you that he'd take care of me.

PENTHEUS
He who? You're always changing subjects.

DIONYSUS
The god, the son of Zeus, the god of wine,
Of transformations –

PENTHEUS

Transgressions

more like!

DIONYSUS

He takes your insult as a compliment.

PENTHEUS

I'll stop this evil spreading. Close the gates!
Everyone to your homes! Lock fast your doors!

DIONYSUS

A wall or door is nothing to a god.

PENTHEUS

You might think you're wise, but I am wise to you.

DIONYSUS

I am wise to that which is worth knowing.
For instance, this man, who now comes this way,
Has news for you. Don't worry, I'll stay put.

Enter HERDSMAN.

HERDSMAN

Pentheus, protector of our city,
I've come directly from Mount Cithairon
Whose white snow caps glint year round in the sun.
Whose fruitful forests –

PENTHEUS

Yes. And you've news for me, or so I'm told.

HERDSMAN

I saw them sir, up there, our womenfolk
Who have abandoned their own homes and run
Up to the mountains like some psychotic army.
I saw them and have come to tell you of actions
Shocking, brute, beyond all belief.

But first, my lord, I must ask if I might
Have leave to freely tell what I have seen.
I fear the fire of your too royal temper.

PENTHEUS

You are quite free to tell what you have seen.
The just man has no need to fear my wrath,
But as for him who schooled them in their vices
His punishment shall be proportionate
To the scale of our womenfolk's offences.

HERDSMAN

At dawn, as I led my herd of cattle
Towards the mountain pastures, I first saw them;
The women, the Bacchai as some now call them,
Because they cry Iacchus Evoe
When they call upon their god and Iacchus,
I suppose, sounds similar to Bacchus,
And they being plural feminine are called Bacchai.
Sorry. Yes. They were in three companies,
When I saw them first – dawn, in the mountains –
One led by Autonoe, the second
Led by Ino and the third, commanded
By their sister, your own mother, Agave.
When I first saw them, they were all asleep
On beds of oak leaves or just bare earth.
All were calm, all quiet, all seemed so innocent,
Not as you've described them, all drunk with wine,
Dancing wild to the music of the pipe,
Or indulging their desires in the sol-
-itary woods, but, like I said, at peace.
Just then, with a start, Agave awoke,
She'd heard the distant sounds of men and beasts;
Herdsmen and their herds. Us. She woke the others.
They rubbed their eyes, stretched, soon all were standing.
At such a time and place, it was a sight;

Their hair free and wild about their shoulders
And teeming with wild snakes that licked their cheeks.
Those who'd left their newborn babes at home
Took up in their arms wild fawns or the whelps of wolves
Which they suckled to their milk-laden breasts.
All wore wreaths of ivy or of oak leaf.
One took her ivy-covered shaft and struck a rock
And from it sprang a spring of fresh water.
Another dug her shaft into the ground
And out flew a fountain of the god's own wine.
If one wanted milk, she just scratched the earth
With fingers, and the earth flowed with it,
While from each sacred shaft honey poured.
If you'd been there you would now praise this god
Whose rites and rituals you try to stop.
We mountain cattleherds and shepherds met up
To swop tales of the wonders we had seen.
One, who'd just returned from town said,
'Listen my mountain friends, what say you all
That Agave, Pentheus' own mother,
We hunt down from this place to please our lord.'
This seemed a good idea so we hid
Amongst the trees and, in ambush, waited.
When they'd had their fill someone gave the sign,
They came together as one company,
Their shafts aloft, they called in one loud voice:
'Dionysus Iacchus, son of Zeus.'
The whole mountain resounded to their cry,
Or so it seemed. The trees, the wild beasts shook,
The rocks themselves seemed come to life
To the beat of the dance they then began.
All led by Agave who, in her whirl,
Whirled near to me so I jumped to catch her,
But she cried out, 'Sisters, my Bacchai,
These men would make prey of us. Come quick, come
With your ivy-covered shafts attack them.'

We turned and ran for it, for we have heard
How the Bacchai, when their god is with them,
Will eat raw the flesh from still-living beasts.
We escaped but they found our grazing herds.
They slaughtered them with nothing but their hands.
One dragged a calf from its own mother's teat
And tore it, as it bellowed, clean in two,
While others pulled apart whole heifers,
The woods soon seemed a bloody abattoir.
Even one proud-horned bull was dragged to earth,
His flesh, by fingernails, scratched from his bones
And the scrag ends hurled high into the trees.
All done by the hands of girls and women,
And quicker than a wink from a royal eye.
Then, as birds skim the surface of a lake,
They flocked down through the fruit-rich mountain glens,
All our women running in wild rampage,
Across the plains where the broad river flows,
To the low-lying village of Erythrae
Which they fell upon like sworn enemies.
They plundered pots and pans and knives and forks
And wrenched babies from their mothers' breasts
And, without strap, bore all off upon their backs.
The villagers, enraged by these actions,
Seized sticks and stones and fired them at the Bacchai.
But then a sight beyond belief, my Lord,
The shower of sticks and stones drew not one single drop of blood
But the ivy shafts, which our womenfolk fired back,
Felled so many men, those who still stood took flight.
Surely some god must work with them when
Women fight like men and men flee like little girls.
As for the Bacchai, sated, for the moment,
They returned to where we first had seen them,
To where the god had poured forth earth's plenty.
They washed the blood from their hands, their faces
Were licked clean by snakes till their cheeks glowed.

Lord, whoever this god, this spirit is,
His power is great, accept him in your city.
Besides, he's given us the gift of wine,
Without which man desires nor endures not.

CHORUS
Lord, although we too fear to speak too freely,
We shall speak all the same:
There is no greater god than Dionysus.

PENTHEUS
This Bacchic evil closes in on me,
Like a forest fire the wind fans this way.
It would consume the city, but it won't.
I will not be made a fool of in the eyes of all the world.
Go summon up the heavy infantry,
The light infantry and all men with horses.
I'll make war against these so-called Bacchai.
I'll not be defied by my own women.

DIONYSUS
Though you'll not take my advice, Pentheus,
And despite the way that you have treated me,
I'll say this to you one last time:
Do not make war upon a god.
Do not threaten a god with force.
Keep calm, keep peaceful, keep your head.
Dionysus will not let his Bacchai
Be forced down from the mountain.

PENTHEUS
If you wish to keep your head,
Then keep your big mouth shut.

DIONYSUS
I'd offer this god sacrifice,
Not sacrifice my office and myself.
Man, like an ass, can't dodge the driver's stick.

PENTHEUS
I'll make a sacrifice alright:
I sacrifice our women's blood
Upon the altar of Mount Cithairon.

DIONYSUS
You'll be destroyed by unarmed women.

PENTHEUS
Why must you always have the final word?

DIONYSUS
Must I? Really? That's the first I've heard.

PENTHEUS
What am I even doing here with you?

DIONYSUS
Friend, perhaps there is something I could do.

PENTHEUS
You think I'll be the subject of some foreign rule.

DIONYSUS
I'll lead them to you without force, you fool.

PENTHEUS
I've had enough for one day of your tricks.

DIONYSUS
A trick? I'm offering to save your neck.

PENTHEUS
You want to save your wild, dancing whores.

DIONYSUS
They're but the symptom, the god is the cause.

PENTHEUS
I've had enough of your god, leave me be!
My armour! Quick, I must go –

DIONYSUS

Ahhhhh, I see
You want to see them in their savage state?

PENTHEUS
I would, I would, I would give my weight in gold to see.

DIONYSUS
Since when have you nurtured such desires?

PENTHEUS
It would, of course, distress me though to see them drunk.

DIONYSUS
But such a sight would be such sweet distress.

PENTHEUS
If I could sit in silence midst the pines.

DIONYSUS
If you go as a spy, they'll hunt you down.

PENTHEUS
Well then, I'll go and watch them openly.

DIONYSUS
So, you agree? You'll let me take you there?

PENTHEUS
Take me there, take me there without delay.

DIONYSUS
First you'll need a dress of eastern linen.

PENTHEUS
Openly? Yet you'd have me hide my sex?

DIONYSUS
If they found a man there, they would kill him.

PENTHEUS
You're right. I've always thought you wise.

DIONYSUS
I'm inspired by Dionysus himself.

PENTHEUS
So, how best might we execute this plan?

DIONYSUS
First we'll go inside and I'll help you change.

PENTHEUS
Change? From man to woman? I'd be ashamed.

DIONYSUS
You must transform yourself if you're to see.

PENTHEUS
What type of dress did you say I must wear?

DIONYSUS
An ankle-length. I'll curl your hair as well.

PENTHEUS
And that will be enough, or not, you think?

DIONYSUS
You'll need a shawl for your head and shoulders.

PENTHEUS
And then, then I can go see them?

DIONYSUS
With deerskin and sacred shaft, you'll be the part.

PENTHEUS
But I can't let myself become a woman.

DIONYSUS
If you use force, blood will spill, and not their blood.

PENTHEUS
You're right. You're right. First I should observe them.

DIONYSUS
Through a veil shall you see the truth unveiled.

PENTHEUS
But how can I pass through the streets unseen?

DIONYSUS
I will take you by deserted back streets.

PENTHEUS
And they must not laugh at me, the Bacchai.

DIONYSUS
Let's go in –

PENTHEUS
                        And I'll decide what I must do?

DIONYSUS
Of course, it's entirely up to you.

PENTHEUS
And I will decide to take them by force,
If I decide against this plan of yours.

DIONYSUS
You are the king. You are Pentheus –

Exit PENTHEUS.

        – no more.
We have him wriggling in the hunter's net.
It is my Bacchai who shall dispense the justice.
Dionysus is at hand, my Asiatic friends,
And he shall be revenged upon this Pentheus.
For it's he who drives him out of his mind,
For surely sane he'd never wear a woman's dress,
And in that dress parade himself along
The teeming thoroughfares of his own city.
He'll pay for his derision of the God,
First with ridicule, and then with death.
But now I must go help him change himself
Into that form in which he'll go to Hades,
Murdered by the hand of his own mother.
He'll learn the nature of this son of Zeus;
The sweetest and most fearsome of the gods.

Exit DIONYSUS after PENTHEUS.

CHORUS
Soon shall we know again
The night-long dance;
Silver moonlit feet,
Head, in bliss, flung back
To the icy air.
A fawn at play in meadows,
Far from the hunter's net,
And shouts,
And straining bloodhounds,
But by a river bank
Free ranging
Like a breeze,
Stiffening to a wind,
In peace from men.
Green shoots sprout in a dark forest.

What is true wisdom?
What is beauty?
What could be better
Than in your hand to hold
Your enemy's fate?
Beauty is always truth.

Slow but unerring move the gods
Against the heedless man.
The man who worships not the gods,
Nor their bounty,
Nor their beauty,
But his own will.
Though the silks of time might veil for a while,
He shall learn through madness in the end.
He who disbelieves,
He who does not respect the gods,
He who seeks power through his own will
And flies in the face
Of the customs and beliefs of his own race,
Shall all be hunted down.
Little does it cost to learn
The little that the gods
Desire of us.
It was known in the beginning
It is the rock of custom
And of law.
It is the weave of our world.

What is true wisdom?
What is beauty?
What could be better
Than in your hand to hold
Your enemy's fate?
Beauty is always truth.

Joy of the storm endured.
And the harbour safely reached.

Joy of hardship overcome.
Joy of striving for wealth and power.
Joy of hope. Joy of dreams,
Fulfilled or unfulfilled.
And most blessed he who takes his joy
In the simple detail of the day by day –

Enter DIONYSUS.

DIONYSUS

Come Pentheus, time to see what you should not,
To rush in where you should most fear to tread.
Come out of the house and reveal yourself
Transformed into a Bacchic celebrant.

Enter PENTHEUS dressed as a Bacchic woman. He is attended by his SERVANT.

PENTHEUS

I seem to see two suns in the sky
And two cities, two wholly different worlds
One up here in light, in the imagination,
The other –

He swoons. DIONYSUS supports him.

And you somehow seem to me a bull,
I can now see two horns upon your head.
Were you a bull before? You are one now.
Was I blind before but now see clear?

DIONYSUS

You see things as you should see things.
You have made a deal with Dionysus
And he is with you now.

PENTHEUS

And how do I look? As fair as Ino?
Or even my own mother, Agave?

DIONYSUS

You're the equal of them both in beauty.
But wait, a lock of hair has wriggled free,
Come here and I will slip it back in place.

PENTHEUS

It must have fallen when I was inside,
Dancing up and down and being a Bacchai.

DIONYSUS

Hold still your head and let me fix it.

PENTHEUS

I place myself entirely in your hands.

DIONYSUS

The ribbons on your dress are undone too,
The pleats hang crooked and your slip shows.

PENTHEUS

You're right, I have become a bit undone.
Do everything that needs be done to me.

DIONYSUS

You'll surely count me as a friend for life,
When you see the Bacchai at their play.

PENTHEUS

The stick? The sacred ivy-covered shaft?
Should I hold it in my right hand or the left
To play the part convincingly?

DIONYSUS

The right, and raise your right arm and left foot.
Together. The change in you is striking.

PENTHEUS

I feel as though I had the strength
To bear Mount Cithairon itself upon my back.

DIONYSUS

Now that you're thinking straight, you can
Do that which you were destined for.

PENTHEUS

Well let us get some crowbars then
To lever loose the mountain.

DIONYSUS

You'd destroy the home of the mountain nymphs,
And the dark woods where Pan plays on his pipes.

PENTHEUS

Yes, you're right, we should not resort to force.
We shall simply observe them from the pines.

DIONYSUS

But you must choose with utmost care your hiding place,
Since it's by deceit you choose to watch them.

PENTHEUS

Now that I am changed, I think of them as birds
Who in their woodland lovenests coo and sigh.

DIONYSUS

Perhaps you'll catch a lovebird or she you?

PENTHEUS

Now lead me through my city's broadest thoroughfares
For I'm the only man who dares this deed.

DIONYSUS

You alone shall bear your city's burden,
And you alone shall undergo this trial.
Now come, I'll lead you to the place,
Though someone else must bring you home –

PENTHEUS

My mother?

DIONYSUS
The world shall witness your return aloft.

PENTHEUS
Aloft in triumph? Let's go straight there then.

DIONYSUS
Held high by your mother.

PENTHEUS

You're flattering me.

DIONYSUS
The truth.

PENTHEUS
I'll only get what I deserve.

Exit PENTHEUS and SERVANT.

DIONYSUS
You're a terrifying man, Pentheus.
And such will be the terror of your end,
Report of it shall spread through all the world.
Agave, daughters of Cadmus, my Bacchai,
Raise up your arms and now receive this man
Whom I deliver to his destiny.
For Dionysus shall prevail,
Though the how and when, only time will tell.

Exit DIONYSUS.

CHORUS
Go you hounds of Hecate,
Go to the mountain,
To where the daughters of old Cadmus dance.

41

Drive out of mind
This man in woman's clothing,
Who seeks to spy upon your mysteries.
His mother shall see him first,
She'll call to the other Bacchai:
'Why has this man
Come to the mountain, women,
But to hunt us down?
Look at him! Look at him! Look at him!
What beast gave birth to him?
Perhaps a mountain lioness,
Or some gorgon.
For surely such monstrosity's
Not from a woman born.'

Go justice, go!
Manifest your wrath.
Go sword of blood
And cut the throat
Of the heedless son
Of earth-born, snake-skinned Echion!

Look at him who disbelieves,
Look at him who does not respect the gods
But, with a desperate fury,
Does battle with the Bacchai and his mother!
Look at him who thinks himself
Stronger than a god!
He'll be driven first out of his mind,
Then driven to his death.
Give to the gods, that which is their due.
Know that your life is dust
And you shall live in peace.

I seek the wisdom of the wise,
But greater still my hunger and my thirst
For a life well lived,
And free from pain.

And such peace is only to be found
If we live both night and day
With an aspect towards the heavens.

Go justice, go!
Manifest your wrath.
Go sword of blood
And cut the throat
Of the heedless son
Of earth-born, snake-skinned Echion!

Come to us now, Dionysus,
Come to us as bull,
Or many-headed serpent,
Or fire-breathing lion,
With your Bacchai hunt the gorgon down,
Hold a mirror to this woman/man
And petrify him in your glass
Then shatter him, shatter him, shatter him.

Enter SERVANT.

SERVANT
O my city and my home once most blessed
And my people grown from the serpent's teeth
Sown by our old king Cadmus!
Though I am but a slave, I weep for you,
And me, since slaves must share their master's fate.

CHORUS
What is it? You have news from the mountain?

SERVANT
Pentheus, son of Echion, is dead.

CHORUS
Dionysus you are made manifest.

SERVANT

What are you saying?

CHORUS

Dionysus has heard us, he has come.

SERVANT

How can you say this?

CHORUS

There is no greater god than Dionysus.

SERVANT

You rejoice in my master's death?

CHORUS

We are strangers here and we sing out loud:
Evoe! Evoe!
We fear no more the justice of the West.

SERVANT

You think there's no men left to rule here?
You think you've no need to fear another's wrath?

CHORUS

Dionysus, Dionysus rules me.
He, not any man, is my king and country.

SERVANT

As foreigners one might just excuse you,
But to praise a wrong is a greater wrong.

CHORUS

He was an unjust man bent on injustice.
But tell us, tell us how he met his death.

SERVANT

The river crossed, the city far behind,
We began to climb the slopes of Cithairon.

Pentheus, the foreign priest and myself,
For though his senses had departed him,
I had not; I served him still.
We soon found ourselves in dark woods.
With soft step and in silence we went on,
So we might observe without being observed.
Soon we saw a glen encircled by tall cliffs,
Refreshed by streams, overshadowed with pines,
And there our women, the Bacchai played.
Some to their battered shafts bound fresh ivy,
Others, like fillies freed from the yoke, danced
And sang songs of Dionysus to each other.
But Pentheus was still dissatisfied and said,
'My foreign friend, from where I sit
I can't see all that these Bacchai women do,
But if I climbed a towering pine upon that cliff,
Then I could see clearly all their mysteries.'
So the foreigner did a most amazing thing:
He reached and touched the topmost branch
Of the tallest pine and pulled it down, down,
Down until the tip which once touched heaven,
Now touched earth; the tree primed, a loaded bow,
A giant arching hemisphere described,
As if by a compass, in the air perfectly.
And this foreigner, this priest did it all by hand.
Surely no mortal could do such a thing.
Then, with care, he put Pentheus on top,
And let the tree spring back up again.
Once more it touched the heavens but, this time,
My master touched the lofty heavens too
And was quite visible to one and all.
And just as his perch became apparent,
I saw the foreign priest had disappeared.
And a voice rang out from the sky and said:
'Here is the man who dared deny Me,
My mysteries and you, now punish him.'

So spoke Dionysus. A bolt of light
Then blazed a line from heaven down to earth.
Silent went the sky, and quite still the air,
Not one single wild beast made a sound.
The women first seemed not to understand,
They stood stock-still, and looked to see who spoke.
Then came the voice again so that this time
There was no doubting the will of the god.
They flew forth like a flock of doves unleashed,
The Bacchai as one body, across stream
And rock and grass, borne on the wind of a god.
They found the tree in which my master sat.
First they fired stones at him and, when this failed,
Some pulled down branches which they hurled at him,
While others fired their sacred shafts up at the tree.
Pentheus, their quarry, was now cornered.
And though, for the moment, he was still out of range,
He had abandoned all hope of escape.
The Bacchai next pulled down great boughs of oak
To lever up the roots of the mighty pine.
But all these efforts were to no avail,
So Agave shouted to the women:
'Come gather round the trunk of this great pine,
Claw its flesh, flay it, bring to ground the beast
Who dares to spy upon our mysteries.'
A thousand hands tore at the tree.
It shuddered, groaned, cracked then crashed to earth,
And with it down fell Pentheus
Who, as he fell, howled at his fate:
He knew what evil must now be performed.
His mother was the first to fall on him,
Frantically, from his face, he pulled his shawl
So she might recognise him,
He touched her cheek, he implored her,
'It is me, mother, your son, Pentheus,
Pentheus whom you bore to Echion

46

Have mercy, mother, do not kill me,
For all that I've done wrong I'm still your son.'
She stopped. She smiled. And then she licked her lips.
Her eyes sharp and shining stared straight through him.
She saw him not, nor heard his fevered words.
She heard only the command of Dionysus.
She placed her hands around his upper arm,
Put her foot upon his chest, and twisted
Off his arm as one might a chicken's wing.
The God must have given her the strength. Then
Ino, like a scavenger, was at him,
Scratching at his flesh, soon too Autonoe,
Then the whole marauding horde of Bacchai,
His dying death's howl joining with their shout
To form one long single ululation.
One carried an arm, another a foot
Which still wore a bloodstained shoe.
They tossed his flesh into the air for joy,
His ribs, picked clean, were used to beat the drum,
The women danced wild and wet with the blood
Of my master, whose body now lies strewn
On rock and tree and through the mountain glens.
And for leading the Bacchai in their hunt,
His mother for her trophy seized his head,
Which seemed to her to be a lion's head,
And, skewering it upon her sacred shaft,
She left her sisters to their crazy dance,
To march down triumphant from the mountain,
Back to her city, calling on the god,
Her fellow hunter, partner in her crime,
The giver of gifts, whose gifts must now be tears.
I'll go now before Agave arrives.
The greatest wisdom is humility,
It is the greatest gift the gods give us;
Most wise the man who uses it.

CHORUS

Dance to the drumbeat,
Celebrate the fate
Of the heedless, headstrong Pentheus,
Who swopped a beard for a dress;
His head is now hoist high
Upon the deadly shaft of Dionysus.
The bull has led him down to Hades.
What fame this victory brings,
What tears, what wild lamentation,
Sweet agony that wreathes
The mother's hand
In her own child's blood.

Look! Agave! She comes towards us.
On her way back to the city.
Her eyes are wild and staring.

AGAVE

Look my Asian Bacchai, look!
I bring down from the mountain
A fresh-cut fruit of the vine.
Our hunt has been most fruitful.
    Pause.
Look what I have caught, women!
The cub of some lioness.
Why do you not look at him?

CHORUS

Where did you catch him, Agave?

AGAVE

Upon the mountain.

CHORUS

                                        But how?

AGAVE

With our bare hands, that's how,
We caught him and slaughtered him.

CHORUS

All of you?

AGAVE

                   I was the first.
Happy, blessed Agave.
Listen, hear the Bacchai sing.

CHORUS

Who then struck him after you?

AGAVE

Ino and Autonoe,
The daughters of old Cadmus,
And my sisters in the hunt.
Come, women, and feast with me.

CHORUS

With you? Where? Feast on what?

AGAVE

This lion was a young one;
His cheeks are soft to touch,
His hair is long and golden.

CHORUS

His hair might make him seem
Like some sort of animal.

AGAVE

Dionysus' aim is true,
He led us to our prey.

CHORUS

Our God is a hunter.

AGAVE

Do you not all honour me?

CHORUS

We honour you.
We honour you.

AGAVE

As will all the city,
Look at them, they're all amazed.

CHORUS

But your son Pentheus?

AGAVE

He too will honour me;
I hunted and I caught a lion cub.
Does this head not appear to you
A thing of greatest wonder?

CHORUS

We see, poor woman, we see
The true nature of your prize.

AGAVE

Come friends, come all of you and honour us.
Look at what the daughters of old Cadmus
Have caught and killed upon Mount Cithairon.
Not with the sharp-tipped Thessalian spear,
Nor with a hunting net, but with our hands –
White blades which carved him up. Let no huntsman
Ever brag of catching beasts with weapons:
With our bare hands, I said, we cut him down
And tore his limbs clean out of their sockets.
Where is my father? Let him come and see.
And my son Pentheus? Let him go place
A ladder up against our house and fix
This trophy to a pillar's pinnacle.

Enter CADMUS followed by SOLDIERS who carry the remains of
PENTHEUS.

CADMUS

This way. Lay him there by his ruined home,
All that I could find of his remains,
Torn into a thousand pieces and strewn
Across the slopes of sacred Cithairon.
I am weary. I had just come back
To the city with Teiresias,
From paying my respects to Dionysus,
When I was told of what my daughters did.
I returned directly to the mountain,
To where I'd heard he had been killed.
I saw Autonoe, mother of Actaeon,
And Ino, still there at their insane sport.
But Agave, they told me, had come here.
Now I see her. A sight to break the heart.

AGAVE

Father, dear, I have something to tell you;
Father you have reared the greatest daughter
A man has ever had. All three of us, I mean,
Though most especially I mean me.
I'm done with weaving, I'm done with the loom,
I've gone to greater things; hunting by hand.
Look, here in my arms, look what I have caught.
Go hang it from our house's highest point.
Go, take it, exult in my victory.
Invite your friends to feast, father, you are blessed.

CADMUS

Pentheus, Penthos, Pentheos, meaning grief.
Bloody deed done by such ill-fated hands.
What a soul you have struck down for your god!
And then you call on us to come and feast?
Your wrong is now my wrong, is all of ours.

The god sought justice, but this goes beyond.
Dionysus has destroyed my house.

AGAVE
Why are the old so seldom satisfied?
Look at him! What's wrong with my family?
If my son was half the hunter that I was –
But he chooses to hunt gods, not wild beasts.
You should talk to him father. Will someone
Go tell him come and see his mother's triumph?

CADMUS
If you could only understand the thing
That you have done, the pain that you would feel.
And yet if you were to remain as you are now,
Though free from pain, your life would be illusion.

AGAVE
What's wrong with you? What have I to grieve for?

CADMUS
First, turn your face up towards the heavens.

AGAVE
And what is it I should see up there?

CADMUS
Does it appear the same or is it changed?

AGAVE
It's the same and yet brighter than before.

CADMUS
And your thoughts? Is your mind still running wild?

AGAVE
I don't know what you mean, yet I do feel
Changed from how I was before. I'm clearer.

CADMUS
And you can hear me and answer clearly?

AGAVE
I'm sorry. What were we talking about?

CADMUS
What man was it took you to be his wife?

AGAVE
Echion, who grew from the serpent's teeth.

CADMUS
What name did you give the son you bore him?

AGAVE
Pentheus was the name we gave our son.

CADMUS
And whose head are you holding in your arms?

AGAVE
The lion's that we hunted down and killed.

CADMUS
Look at it again, tell me what you see.

AGAVE
Ea! Ea!
What am I looking at? What's this I hold?

CADMUS
Look long and carefully and you will see.

AGAVE
I see grief, a grief beyond endurance.

CADMUS
Does this still seem a lion's head to you?

AGAVE

It seems that I hold the head of my son.

CADMUS

And it seems that you are the last to know.

AGAVE

But who killed him? Tell me father.
Why do I hold his head in my accursed arms?

CADMUS

Accursed the day when such a truth be told.

AGAVE

Who killed him? My heart beats like a drum.

CADMUS

You killed him. You and your sisters killed him.

AGAVE

Where? How? In the house? Where did we do it?

CADMUS

Where Actaeon was devoured by his own dogs.

AGAVE

But what evil drove him to Mount Cithairon?

CADMUS

He went there to spy upon your sisters and on you.

AGAVE

But what cause had we to go up there?

CADMUS

You were possessed by Dionysus.

AGAVE

Dionysus? Well he has now dispossessed me truly.

CADMUS

You denied he was a god. He has answered you.

AGAVE

Where's the body of my beloved son?

CADMUS

I've brought down from the mountain what remains.

AGAVE

What have I done? What have these hands done?
Why him? If the God wished to punish me,
Why did my Pentheus have to die?

CADMUS

Just like you, he did not respect the god
And, since he was the last male of my line,
We shall all now share his ruin.
Fruit of your womb, the last fruit of my tree;
Shameful, shocking, black and evil harvest.
Through him my line would have refound its way.
Hope of my house, more a son to me than grandson.
Scourge of the city, he made sure that I
Was respected and revered, and he'd deal
Any scoundrel who defied him tough justice.
But now, though I'm the oldest of the old,
Though I sowed the serpent's teeth which grew
Into the golden summer of this city,
I, the mighty Cadmus, am now nothing,
My line dust, my last years shame and emptiness.
My beloved boy, no more shall you touch
My cheek, put an arm around my shoulder
And say 'What's wrong, old man? Does someone dare
Not show you the respect that you deserve?
Tell me grandfather and I'll see to him.'
But now all that is left is misery
For you, your mother and myself.

Let he who would defy the gods' demands
Look at this piteous death and believe.

CHORUS
Though this man got what he deserved,
We grieve for you now Cadmus, for what you suffer.

AGAVE
Father, give me his body? I must prepare
His body for burial. Where is my son?

CADMUS
Agave, my daughter, you are his killer,
You cannot be the one to bury him.

AGAVE
I have killed him, yes, but I'm his mother still.
I am both the wrong-doer and the wronged.
I have killed part of myself, let me look,
At least, and see what I have done.

CADMUS
Men, bring here what remains of him.
I shudder for you, for what you are to see.

PENTHEUS' remains are presented. AGAVE attempts to reassemble his body.

AGAVE
My son, my lovely son, my Pentheus.
See father, women, all of you see,
See how in so little time all's so changed.
It seems just a moment since to my breast
I held my darling baby boy and laughed
As he bit my nipples with soft milk-teeth,
And I pinched his small button of a nose.
And a moment since he first walked to me
And talked to me. And now he's gone from me.

Bring a cloth, a shroud, let me cover him.
Please let me remember him as he was and
Let me forget that I have ever been.

A shroud. DIONYSUS is revealed in the form of a god.

DIONYSUS
Hear me, hear my cry. Do you not hear it now?
Did I not say, did I not tell you that
This city here would be the first
Of all the western world to cry my cry?
O sweet ululation. Do you not know me still?
In the form of a god I am revealed;
God of the vine, god of dramatic rites
God of the transformation from the humdrum
To the wild abandon of the play.
Look at them, do they not seem abandoned now?
And you? Was not your disbelief suspended?
Just a bit?
I can conjure worlds in the imagination
And destroy those worlds.

The stage gradually returns to its original bare state.

Do not deny me.
Do not insult me. Do not deride my arts,
My gifts. Do not attempt to silence me.
Do not think that if you lock me up,
I will go away. Look at Pentheus,
For such shameful acts, shameful was his end.
Do not think that I am not important.
I am part of you. I am in your mind.
As for you, Agave, leave this place now.
With your sisters you shall live in exile,
Impoverished and in perpetuity.
Go take your pollution from this city.

Cadmus, your house is dust, your line is over.
You only ever played the part of a believer
Putting on the appearance of a faith
To further your own family's interests.
You too must now leave this city.
Exiled you shall take on a serpent's form,
You and your wife Harmonia,
So shall you both live belly to the earth,
Dust in mouth, beast-like in shape and nature,
Until delivered up to the hereafter.
So shall it be, for I, Dionysus,
The son of Zeus, am a god eternal.

CADMUS
Forgive us, we have done you wrong but we repent.

DIONYSUS
You believe, but your belief comes too late.

CADMUS
But is this death not punishment enough?

DIONYSUS
You have not shown due honour to a god.

CADMUS
Should a god be as vengeful as a man?

DIONYSUS
Gods are not vengeful, gods are, and men must accept.

AGAVE
Ai, it is so, old man, we must accept
Our punishment. We have no choice except
To do it with our heads held high and live
The remainders of our lives courageously;
Out of the grace and out of the sight of the gods!

DIONYSUS

Go then. What is destined cannot be deferred.

DIONYSUS is gone.

CADMUS

What evil has befallen us, my child?
You, your sisters and myself all ruined?
I must now go to barbarous lands,
An old man forced to build his life once more,
And there I and my wife Harmonia
Must take the form of serpents in the wild.
Powerless to prevent that which is foretold,
And powerless to end it all in sweet death.

AGAVE

Exiled from our home and one another.

CADMUS

Why do you put your arm around me child,
As the cygnet clings to the old dying swan?

AGAVE

How will I be happy far from my home?

CADMUS

I do not know, child. I am little help.

AGAVE

Farewell my city,
Farewell my home,
Farewell my wedding bed,
…My son.
Show us the way Asian women,
Show us the way to bitter exile,
Far from the mountain,
To where ivy shaft nor dance nor drum reminds…

Exit AGAVE and CADMUS.

CHORUS
The gods take many forms,
The gods move in strange ways,
That which seemed, does not transpire
And that which did not, does.
This is what transpired here.
Turn out the lights.

The End